Table of Contents

1. How's My Emotional Sobriety?..1
2. Describing Myself...3
3. Photographs That Tell a Story..9
4. Letting the Body Speak..12
5. Exploring Relationship and Life Traumas...15
6. Self Medicating With Food or Other Substances or Behaviors?.........................21
7. How is Old Pain Being Lived Out in My Relationships Today?..........................25
8. How is Trauma Impacting My Parenting?...27
9. Feeling the Feelings that Went On Hold: Processing Grief.................................31
10. Exploring Depression and Anxiety..38
11. Taming the Wild Beast: Processing Anger..45
12. Finding Forgiveness..53
13. Building Resilience..58
14. Finding Ways to Feel Good Naturally...63
15. Building My Recovery Network...65
16. Making Changes: Exploring Life Roles...67

This workbook is designed to go with my book *Emotional Sobriety: From Relationship Balance to Resilience and Balance,* not to be used on it's own. Emotional Sobriety is available everywhere books are sold and through my web site tiandayton.com. This workbook not a substitute for therapy nor does it give any advice or direction beyond that of any book. The writer cannot assume any responsibility for interpretations made.

Dear Reader,

Welcome to this workbook on emotional sobriety. This workbook includes questions, self assessments and journaling exercises designed to help you to develop the skills of emotional sobriety. Work on sections in order or in whatever way best suits your needs. As you use this workbook remember a few things:

- *Go at your own pace: No one is watching or grading you, do this book in whatever way feels right to you*
- *Be open and honest: This book is for your eyes only unless you choose to share it. Writing is a wonderful way to get to know yourself and what's inside of you and it even elevates the immune system, so enjoy the process.*
- *Use this along with the book, Emotional Sobriety: From Relationship Trauma Resilience and Balance, rather than on its own, it will be much more valuable to you if you have read or are reading the book.*
- *This workbook is not a substitute for therapy or professional help of any kind nor for the community and good orderly direction of Twelve Step Programs. It works best in conjunction with any of these. Do as many or as few exercises as you wish, in any order that you wish. Use this book entirely at your own pace and discretion.*

If you are a therapist using this with clients I recommend that you ask the client to follow the same process of reading the book and doing exercises that feel right to them then sharing and processing in one to one or group.

In addition to the work book I have three downloadable CDs, one a guided relaxation so that you will be able to learn the skills of restoring your own state of calm. Use this guided relaxation any time you want to take a restorative break or just before bed. As you use it over and over again, you will gradually internalize the skills of self soothing and self regulation that we talk about throughout the Emotional Sobriety. You will learn to access and expand that pool of calm within you so that you can return to it throughout your day and you will learn how to enter a meditative state. The other imageries are designed to give you an experience of connecting with your inner world, processing and releasing anxiety and pain and allowing in more peaceful and pleasant emotions. Do not use these imageries if you are driving a car.

If you wish to learn more on Emotional Sobriety by signing up for teleseminars on emotional sobriety or to receive a free quarterly newsletter just sign up on tiandayton.com.

Enjoy the process and all the best,

Tian

Chapter 1
How's My Emotional Sobriety?

In this chapter you will be exploring your level of emotional sobriety.
Instructions: Rate Your Answers from One to Ten.

> Key: This is a self-test designed to increase your awareness about your own level of emotional sobriety in all of these relevant categories. Your numeric rating is not a grade, just an indication for you of where your work might lie.

1. How much can you tolerate the strength of your own emotions?

    1 2 3 4 5 6 7 8 9 10

2. How much do you live in emotional extremes?

    1 2 3 4 5 6 7 8 9 10

3. How much do you live in emotional balance?

    1 2 3 4 5 6 7 8 9 10

4. How good are you at translating your strong feelings into words?

    1 2 3 4 5 6 7 8 9 10

5. How much do you use substances (drugs, alcohol) as mood regulators?

    1 2 3 4 5 6 7 8 9 10

6. How much do you use of compulsive behaviors as mood regulators?

    1 2 3 4 5 6 7 8 9 10

7. How much unresolved pain from your past do you carry?

   1   2   3   4   5   6   7   8   9   10

8. How much does that pain hold you back in your life?

   1   2   3   4   5   6   7   8   9   10

9. In your intimate relationships?

   1   2   3   4   5   6   7   8   9   10

10. In your work life?

    1   2   3   4   5   6   7   8   9   10

11. How much depression do you feel?

    1   2   3   4   5   6   7   8   9   10

12. How much anxiety do you experience?

    1   2   3   4   5   6   7   8   9   10

13. How comfortable are you in your body?

    1   2   3   4   5   6   7   8   9   10

14. How much does your body carry emotional pain?

    1   2   3   4   5   6   7   8   9   10

Chapter 2
Describing Myself

In this chapter you will be exploring the influences of your early environment and relationships and how you experienced them. You will also be doing some journaling exercises that allow you to make a connection with yourself while growing up, giving the child, adolescent or growing person within you a voice. As always throughout this book, do as much or as little as you wish.

Describe the home you grew up in.

_____
_____
_____

What was the feeling atmosphere?

_____
_____
_____

How did you fit in?

_____
_____
_____

How was discipline handled?

_____
_____
_____

Did you feel special? Explain.

_____

_____

_____

Did you feel understood? Explain.

_____

_____

_____

How were holiday rituals handled in your home?

_____

_____

_____

What was the best thing about your home?

_____

_____

_____

What was something that bothered you?

_____

_____

_____

How did your parents get along?

_____

_____

_____

Were they affectionate with each other?

_____
_____
_____

Did they fight a lot?

_____
_____
_____

How did that affect you?

_____
_____
_____

How did your mother feel about you?

_____
_____
_____

How did that make you feel about yourself?

_____
_____
_____

How did your father feel about you?

_____
_____
_____

How did that make you feel about yourself?

_____
_____
_____

Describe your siblings, how many were you and how were your relationships?

_____
_____
_____

Who are other family members such as grandparents, aunts, uncles, cousins or pets who where important to you and why?

_____
_____
_____

Did you have a favorite pet? Describe your relationship.

_____
_____
_____

Did you feel you could bring problems to your parents and talk them over?

_____
_____
_____

How did that conversation look?

_____
_____
_____

How did you learn to regulate your emotions, how were your emotions handled and how was self regulation modeled for you?

_____
_____
_____

Describe a cozy memory, routines that you remember that made you feel content and secure.

_____
_____
_____

Describe things that happened that tended to throw you off balance.

_____
_____
_____

Describe ways in which independence and individuation was supported in your home?

_____
_____
_____

Describe ways in which independence and individuation was discouraged in your home.

_____
_____
_____

Journaling Exercises

Imagine someone who knows you well and reverse roles with them in your mind. Speaking AS them, describe yourself from their point of view, through their eyes (e.g., My name is Harry and I want to tell you about my daughter, Tian).

_____
_____
_____
_____
_____

Reverse roles in your mind with someone else and write a journal entry describing you (e.g., I am Brandt and I am describing Tian, she seems to me, etc.).

_____
_____
_____
_____
_____

Reverse roles in your mind with ANYONE you wish to do this exercise with such as a beloved grandmother, teacher or firend and write a journal entry describing you (e.g., I am Grammie and I am describing Tian, she seems to me, etc.). Repeat process with father.

_____
_____
_____
_____
_____

Chapter 3
Photographs That Tell a Story

In this chapter you will be scrap booking, looking for photo graphs that tell a story and allowing them to speak to, for and about you. You will be letting pictures come alive and talk to you.

Find photographs that speak to you in some way either of yourself at any stage of your life, family members, friends or pets. Paste them onto these pages or scan them onto a separate piece of paper and answer the following questions. Answer as many or as few questions as you wish.

What does this picture evoke for you?

_____
_____
_____

Describe the people in this photograph in a line or two.

_____
_____
_____

What were you feeling on the inside at the time it was taken?

_____
_____
_____

What does this picture mean to you?

_____
_____
_____

What is the voice inside of you saying in this picture?

_____
_____
_____

What do you imagine the voices inside of others in this picture are saying?

_____
_____
_____

Who in this picture do you need to talk to and what do you want to say?

_____

_____

_____

Who do you feel has something to say to you? Say what you imagine that is.

_____

_____

_____

What does this picture mean or symbolize to you?

_____

_____

_____

Chapter 4
Letting the Body Speak

In this chapter you will be allowing your body to have a voice, you will let the story that your body knows emerge through writing.

The Emotional Body: How Our Bodies Process Emotion

Where do you experience your emotions in your body?

_____

_____

_____

Do you have any area of your body in which you experience your stress? (I.e.: headaches, stomach, back pain, excessive muscle tension)

_____

_____

_____

If that part of your body had a voice, what would it like to say?

_____

_____

_____

If that part of you could take an action or actions, what would it like to do?

_____

_____

_____

Can you identify any area of your body in which you feel numb?

_____
_____
_____

Describe the numbness, does it have a color?

_____
_____
_____

Does it have a texture? A sound?

_____
_____
_____

If it could say a word or a few words what would they be?

_____
_____
_____

If it could take an action, what would it be?

_____
_____
_____

Journal as a part of your body that still carries numbness or pain or strong emotions of any kind.
(I.e.: I am Emily's stomach and I....)

Chapter 5
Exploring Relationship and Life Traumas

In this chapter you will be exploring life traumas and how they may have set up patterns of thinking, feeling and behavior that continue to impact your life. You will be creating a time line of your life issues so that you can identify where and when they impacted your life and whether or not they became the origin of repeating patterns throughout your life.

SELF-TEST /SOCIOMETRY FOR TRAUMA RELATED SYMPTOMS
(© Tian Dayton, *Trauma and Addiction*)

> Key: This is a self-test designed to increase your awareness about your own level of emotional sobriety in all of these relevant categories. Your numeric rating is not a grade, just an indication for you of where your work might lie.

1. Do you feel emotionally numb or out of touch with you emotions in certain areas of your life?

    Never *Now & Then* *Sometimes* *Often* *Always*
    □ □ □ □ □

2. Do you have bouts of depression and despair that do not resolve themselves within a reasonable length of time?

    Never *Now & Then* *Sometimes* *Often* *Always*
    □ □ □ □ □

3. Are you constantly waiting for the bottom to fall out; do you mistrust calm and orderly living?

    Never *Now & Then* *Sometimes* *Often* *Always*
    □ □ □ □ □

4. Do you tend to go from 0 – 10 in your emotional life and have trouble staying on middle ground?

    Never *Now & Then* *Sometimes* *Often* *Always*
    □ □ □ □ □

5. Do you feel you recreate the same problems over and over again getting stuck in the same place?

   Never ☐   Now & Then ☐   Sometimes ☐   Often ☐   Always ☐

6. Do you have trouble identifying what what you really feel?

   Never ☐   Now & Then ☐   Sometimes ☐   Often ☐   Always ☐

7. Do your feelings evidence themselves as body sensations such as headaches, stomachaches, backaches, instead of as conscious feelings?

   Never ☐   Now & Then ☐   Sometimes ☐   Often ☐   Always ☐

8. Do you have larger-than-appropriate emotional reactions when some sort of situation or interaction triggers you?

   Never ☐   Now & Then ☐   Sometimes ☐   Often ☐   Always ☐

9. Do you have trouble taking in help and support from others?

   Never ☐   Now & Then ☐   Sometimes ☐   Often ☐   Always ☐

10. Do you isolate and have trouble being in community or intimate relationships?

    Never ☐   Now & Then ☐   Sometimes ☐   Often ☐   Always ☐

11. Do you feel guilty when your life improves?

    Never ☐   Now & Then ☐   Sometimes ☐   Often ☐   Always ☐

12. Do you self-medicate your feelings or try to alter your mood with drugs?

    Never ☐   Now & Then ☐   Sometimes ☐   Often ☐   Always ☐

13. Do you engage in high-risk behaviors in order to "feel alive"?

    Never ☐   Now & Then ☐   Sometimes ☐   Often ☐   Always ☐

14. Do you experience more anxiety than you feel is normal?

    Never ☐   *Now & Then* ☐   *Sometimes* ☐   *Often* ☐   *Always* ☐

15. Do you find yourself avoiding situations that are reminiscent of previous painful situations?

    Never ☐   *Now & Then* ☐   *Sometimes* ☐   *Often* ☐   *Always* ☐

16. Do you have a hard time envisioning your future?

    Never ☐   *Now & Then* ☐   *Sometimes* ☐   *Often* ☐   *Always* ☐

17. Do you experience flashbacks or nightmares that are reminiscent of your trauma or are otherwise upsetting?

    Never ☐   *Now & Then* ☐   *Sometimes* ☐   *Often* ☐   *Always* ☐

18. Do you experience intrusive thoughts related to your trauma(s)?

    Never ☐   *Now & Then* ☐   *Sometimes* ☐   *Often* ☐   *Always* ☐

Journaling Exercises

Think of a situation, person or relationship dynamic that often triggers you. Within the box below, put words and phrases that describe your feelings at the moments when you feel triggered.

When I get triggered I feel...

What comes to mind when you look at these words and phrases?

_____
_____
_____
_____

What unspoken feelings or words, what unresolved pain from the past might be adding fuel to your present reaction?

_____
_____
_____
_____

Try to separate out and identify which situation from the past causes you to overreact in the present.

_____
_____
_____
_____

Trauma Time Line

Instructions: Recall life situations that you found frightening, painful, disruptive or traumatic and write them on the appropriate times that correspond to your age at the time they occurred.

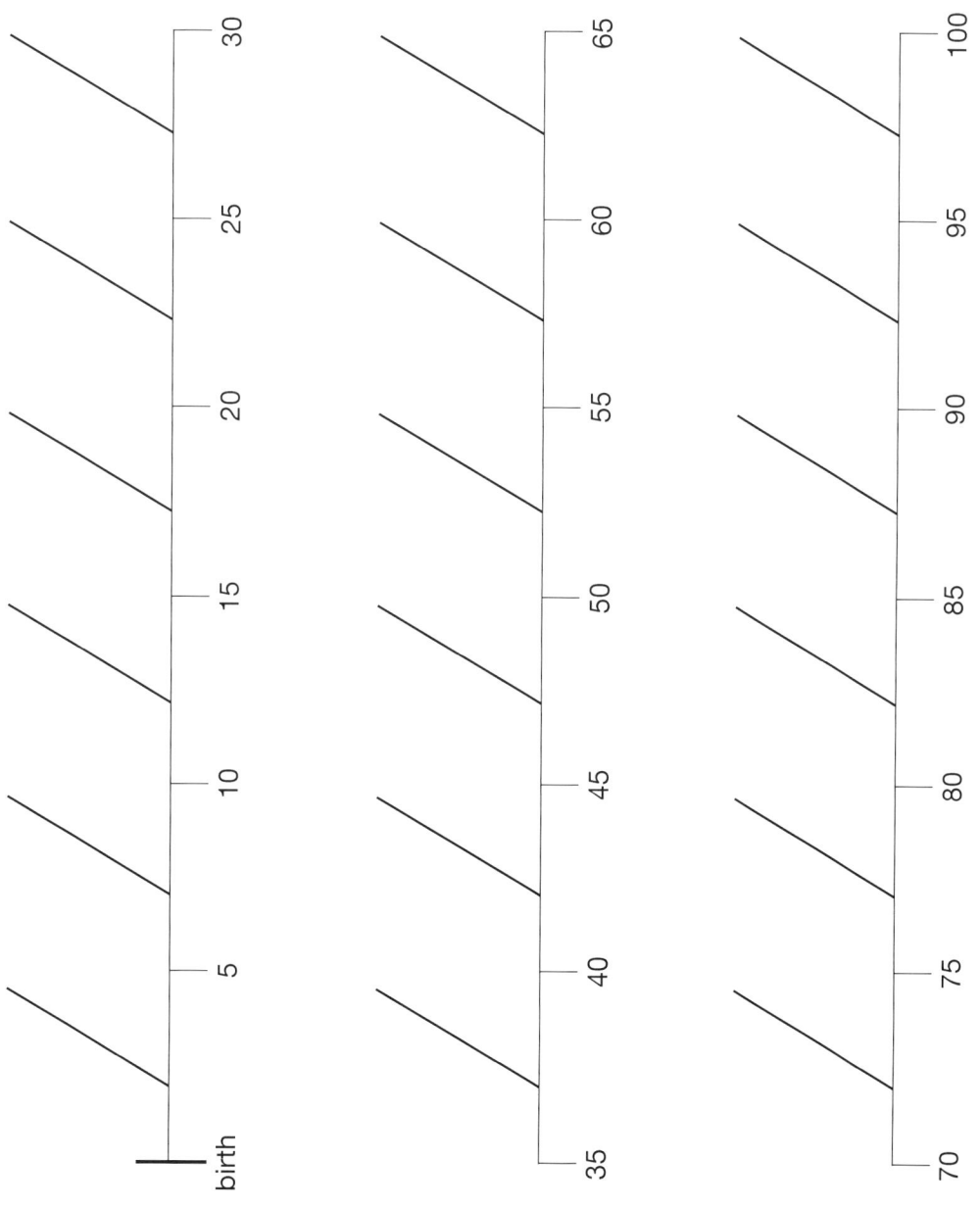

What do you notice about doing this time line?

Do some traumas seem to be piling up at any one point in your life?

Was there a difference in life before the trauma and life after it?

Identify a time in your life before trauma occurred if possible and write a journal entry describing your life at that time.

Do you notice a difference between your life and how you felt about yourself and your relationships before and after trauma? Describe the differences.

Chapter 6
Self Medicating With Food or Other Substances or Behaviors

In this chapter you will be exploring how food was used in your home along with whether or not you use substances or compulsive behaviors to self medicate. This can be filled out for alcohol or other substances, simply put "alcohol" or "drugs" or "sexual acting out" in place of food in questions 9 and on.

1. What was your early experience of nurturing? How much were you held, how much were you in a playpen or crib?

   _____
   _____
   _____

2. What was the feeling atmosphere? Were you nursed or bottle fed?

   _____
   _____

3. When did you start solid food?

   _____
   _____
   _____

4. Were you fed when hungry or on a strict schedule?

   _____
   _____
   _____

5. Did you eat until full?

_____
_____
_____

6. What were your ways of soothing yourself as a baby, toddler and young child?

_____
_____
_____

7. In your household were you overfed, underfed, or allowed to self-regulate?

_____
_____
_____

8. What were your food "relationships"; who did eating or not eating connect you with? How did the family interact around food?

_____
_____
_____

9. How was food (alcohol, drugs, work, money etc.) used in your home (i.e., for comfort, connection, anxiety reduction, reward, punishment, etc.)? Explain.

_____
_____
_____

10. What meanings did food (alcohol, drugs, work, money etc.) have in your house? Explain.

_____
_____
_____

11. How do you use food (alcohol, drugs, work, money etc.) in your own life?

_____
_____
_____

12. What is your eating (alcohol, drugs, work, money etc.) pattern today?

_____
_____
_____

13. What meaning does food (alcohol, drugs, work, money etc.) have in your life today?

_____
_____
_____

14. Do you have trouble saying "no" to yourself or "yes" to yourself when it comes to food (alcohol, drugs, work, money etc.)?

_____
_____
_____

15. What positive or negative impact is food (alcohol, drugs, work, money etc.) having on your life today?

_____
_____
_____

16. At what moments throughout the day do you tend to overeat (drink, use, spend, overdo)?

17. What situations trigger you to overeat (drink, use, spend, overdo)?

18. Does food (alcohol, drugs, work, money etc.) connect you with anyone in particular in your life today?

19. Can you identify a particular moment in your life or situation when you began to overeat (drink, use, spend, overdo)?

20. What would you like your relationship with food (alcohol, drugs, work, money etc.) to look like today?

Chapter 7

How is Old Pain Being Lived Out in My Relationships Today?

In this chapter you will be exploring how emotional, psychological and even physiological pain from the past may being lived out in your life today.

Identify a problematic dynamic, fight or obsessive preoccupation that occurs over and over again in your adult intimate relationships.

_____
_____
_____

Describe the ways in which that dynamic repeats itself.

_____
_____
_____

Describe how you feel, think and behave at those times.

_____
_____
_____

When have you felt that way before and with whom? (note: it may be more than once and with more than one person. It may be a state that repeats itself)

_____
_____
_____

What would you like to say now that you couldn't say then and to whom would you like to say it?

_____
_____
_____

What would you like to do now that you couldn't do then and to or with whom?

_____

_____

_____

What meaning did you make about yourself or intimate relationships at this or these times that you might still be living by today?

_____

_____

_____

Now reverse roles with yourself at that or those original times when you felt hurt, misunderstood or angry and journal as that part of yourself (i.e.: I am Tian, I am 12 years old and I feel…).

_____

_____

_____

_____

_____

_____

Now come back into the present. What do you see now about the repeating dynamic in your relationships today that you didn't see before?

_____

_____

_____

Chapter 8
How is trauma Impacting My Parenting?

In this chapter you will be exploring how your own personal issues may be affecting your parenting and which areas of parenting may be involved.

Identify an issue that you have had or are having with one of your children.

_____
_____
_____

Describe how you feel about what's going on.

_____
_____
_____

Now remember what was going on in your own life when you were at the age that your child with whom you are experiencing problems, is now. (i.e.: If your child is twelve, what was going on in your life at age twelve? This is an *age correspondence reation*.)

_____
_____
_____

Do you see any similarities between what was going on in your life and what you may be feeling is happening for your child right now? (i.e.: are you projecting your own unresolved emotions from that period of your life into that period in your child's life?)

_____
_____
_____

Next ask yourself when you have felt the same way that you're imaging your child is feeling now.

_____

_____

_____

Describe the situation surrounding the feelings.

_____

_____

_____

Do you see any similarity between how you felt then and what you imagine your child is feeling now?

_____

_____

_____

Self Test

Instructions: Which of the following do you identify with and to what extent?

Do you:

Have trouble tolerating your children being rejected by anyone?

Never	Now & Then	Sometimes	Often	Always
☐	☐	☐	☐	☐

Have problems with your own self-regulation that impacts how you deal with your children's ups and downs?

Never	Now & Then	Sometimes	Often	Always
☐	☐	☐	☐	☐

Tend to violate your children's boundaries by being unnecessarily intrusive and overly curious about your child's affairs?

Never	Now & Then	Sometimes	Often	Always
☐	☐	☐	☐	☐

Either read too much into situations that bother your children or block them?

Never	Now & Then	Sometimes	Often	Always
☐	☐	☐	☐	☐

Overprotect your children even when it is not in your children's best interest?

Never	Now & Then	Sometimes	Often	Always
☐	☐	☐	☐	☐

Not know what normal is and consequently have trouble understanding which behaviors to accept or foster as normal in your children and which behaviors to discourage?

Never	Now & Then	Sometimes	Often	Always
☐	☐	☐	☐	☐

Have trouble having relaxed and easy fun with your children?

Never	Now & Then	Sometimes	Often	Always
☐	☐	☐	☐	☐

Have impulsive features that you act out in your parenting?

Never	Now & Then	Sometimes	Often	Always
☐	☐	☐	☐	☐

Feel somewhat different from other families?

Never	Now & Then	Sometimes	Often	Always
☐	☐	☐	☐	☐

Attempt to over control family life and the lives of your children?

Never	Now & Then	Sometimes	Often	Always
☐	☐	☐	☐	☐

Have trouble establishing healthy boundaries with your children, positioning yourself either too close or too far?

Never	Now & Then	Sometimes	Often	Always
☐	☐	☐	☐	☐

Layer your unresolved historical emotions onto your relationships with your children?

Never	Now & Then	Sometimes	Often	Always
☐	☐	☐	☐	☐

How do feel pain from your past might be impacting your parenting?

Which strengths from your upbringing do you feel are helping you in your parenting?

Which weaknesses from your upbringing do you feel might be impacting your parenting?

What are three things you can do to become more comfortable in your relationship with your child? Explain.

1.

2.

3.

Chapter 9

Feeling the Feelings that Went On Hold: Processing Grief

In this chapter you will be allowing yourself to understand and explore the grief process. You will be able to explore *if* and *how* unresolved grief from the past may be impacting your present along with gaining a better understanding of the stages of the grieving process. You will also, through the "Loss Chart" explore how being hurt in the present may be "warming up" old hurts from the past and making the present feel over burdened.

Grief Self Test

Rate your answers to the following questions from one-ten.

1. To what degree do you experience unresolved emotions surrounding this loss?

    1   2   3   4   5   6   7   8   9   10

2. How disruptive was this loss to your daily routines?

    1   2   3   4   5   6   7   8   9   10

3. How much depression do you feel?

    1   2   3   4   5   6   7   8   9   10

4. How much yearning do you feel?

    1   2   3   4   5   6   7   8   9   10

5. How much emotional constriction do you experience?

    1   2   3   4   5   6   7   8   9   10

6. How much sadness do you feel?

    1   2   3   4   5   6   7   8   9   10

7. How much anger do you feel?

   1   2   3   4   5   6   7   8   9   10

8. How much ghosting (continued psychic presence) of the lost person, situation, or part of self do you feel?

   1   2   3   4   5   6   7   8   9   10

9. How much fear of the future do you feel?

   1   2   3   4   5   6   7   8   9   10

10. How much trouble are you having organizing yourself?

    1   2   3   4   5   6   7   8   9   10

11. How uninterested in your life do you feel?

    1   2   3   4   5   6   7   8   9   10

12. How much old, unresolved grief is being activated and remembered as a result of this current issue?

    1   2   3   4   5   6   7   8   9   10

13. How tired do you feel?

    1   2   3   4   5   6   7   8   9   10

14. How much hope do you feel about your life and the future?

    1   2   3   4   5   6   7   8   9   10

15. How much regret do you feel?

    1   2   3   4   5   6   7   8   9   10

16. How much self-recrimination do you feel?

    1   2   3   4   5   6   7   8   9   10

17. How much shame or embarrassment do you feel?

    1   2   3   4   5   6   7   8   9   10

Stages of the Grief Process

On the following lines write a few phrases or sentences that describe your feelings around each stage as they relate to the grief issue(s) that you are exploring.

Numbness and Shut Down (nature's way of preserving us so that we can function)
Describe the feelings that went on hold.

_____
_____
_____
_____
_____

Yearning and Searching
Describe the feelings of longing for what was lost.

_____
_____
_____
_____
_____

Disorganization and Despair

Describe ways in which your life may feel disorganized by your loss and any feelings of sadness or despair that you may be feeling because of that.

_____

_____

_____

_____

_____

Reorganization and Integration

Describe ways in which you feel you are integrating your loss and moving on in your life.

_____

_____

_____

_____

_____

Reinvestment

Describe ways in which you are reinvesting the freed up energy in your current life that you have as a result of having grieved.

_____

_____

_____

_____

_____

Loss Map

In the empty circle on the page write in a loss that you are currently focusing on (i.e., loss of a friend; a break up; death of a loved one; parents' divorce; etc.). On the lines stemming from the box write words or phrases that describe other losses that this loss brings to mind.

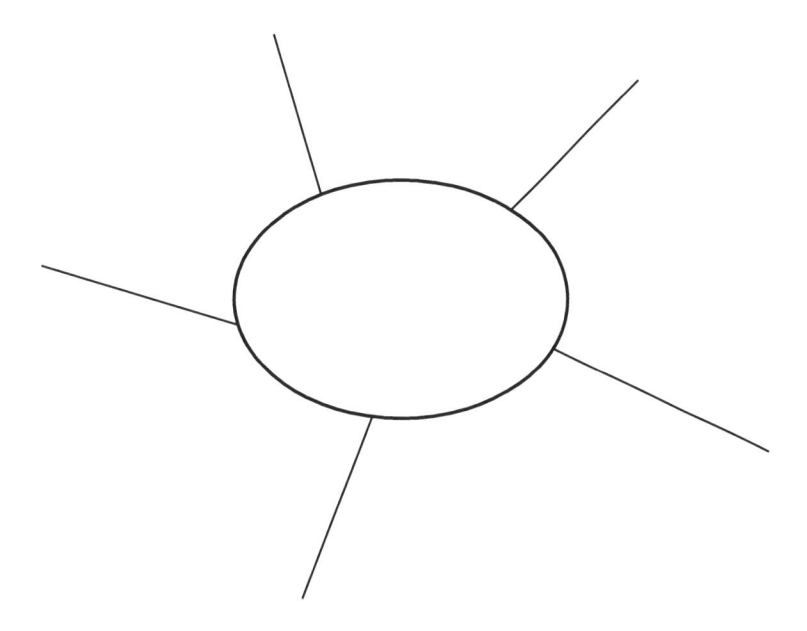

Ask yourself these questions:

What do you notice about your loss or losses that hadn't occurred to you before?

What old losses from the past do you feel might be impacting your life today?

Journaling Exercises

Do whichever exercises you feel drawn to. Use your own extra paper if necessary.

Write a letter to someone.

___

Write a letter to someone who feels lost to you.

___

Write a letter to a part of yourself that feels lost to you.

Journal about a time in your life when you feel you lost.

Journal about a part of your self that still carries pain/anger, yearning or urges to take actions that were stifled in the past.

Chapter 10
Exploring Anxiety and Depression

In this chapter you will be exploring issues with depression and anxiety and allowing those feelings to have a voice. You will also be looking at what times of day, the week, month or year that you experience these feelings most strongly.

At what times of day do you tend to feel depressed or anxious? Put an "X" on the clock at those times of day. Write a short description on the lines below of how you feel at each of those times.

_____
_____
_____
_____
_____
_____
_____

	Morning	Afternoon	Evening
Monday			
Tuesday			
Wednesday			
Thursday			
Friday			
Saturday			
Sunday			

At what times of week do you feel depressed or anxious? Put an "X" at those times. Write a short description or journal of how you feel at each time. Use extra paper if necessary.

_____
_____
_____
_____
_____
_____
_____
_____

At what times of year do you feel depressed or anxious?
Write a short description of how you feel at each time.

January	February	March	April
May	June	July	August
September	October	November	December

Write a journal entry. Reverse roles with some part of your body that feels like it holds your anxiety or depression and write a journal entry as that body part (i.e.: "I am Anna's stomack and I want to scream, I am constantly..." or "I am Larry's legs and I have a lot to say, I am...").

_____
_____
_____
_____
_____
_____
_____
_____
_____
_____
_____
_____
_____
_____
_____
_____
_____
_____
_____
_____

Refer to the clock exercise:

Write a journal entry about how your anxiety or depression feels to you at the particular time/s of day that you experience it most strongly. Journal about the feelings underneath, both rational and irrational (i.e.: I feel filled with fears that have little base in reality, or fears that have some basis but I exaggerate them so much that they paralyze me. Or I feel consumed by an irrational dread of the day, the moment, the future. Just getting going seems overwhelming).

Refer to the calendar exercise:
Write a journal entry about how your anxiety or depression feels to you at the particular time(s) of year that you experience it most strongly. Journal about the feelings underneath, both rational and irrational. (i.e.: around this time of year I get anxious that... or, around this time of year all of these feelings come up...).

How does your anxiety or depression make you think, feel and behave?

_____
_____
_____

My anxious and/or depressed thoughts sound like this in my head:

_____
_____
_____

My anxious and/or depressed feelings are these:

_____
_____
_____

When I get anxious/depressed I feel:

_____
_____
_____

My anxious and/or depressed behaviors are:

_____
_____
_____

When I get anxious/depressed I tend to: (list or share your common actions or behaviors, i.e.: I get sluggish, I isolate, I am easily angered, I get flat, or I get physical symptoms like stomach problems, headaches, muscle tightness, I'm easily triggered, I get irritated over little things and so on)

_____
_____
_____

Chapter 11

Taming the Wild Beast: Processing Anger

In this chapter you will be exploring your feelings of anger in all of its various forms and allowing your anger to have a voice. You will, through the "anger map" come to see how past anger may be getting mixed up with present anger and taking a look at what may lie beneath that. You will also have journaling exercises designed to allow you to explore times in your life when anger may have been a problem and how you might have repaired your feelings of discomfort and disconnection. As always, do as much or as little as you wish.

Anger Self Test

Rate your answers to the following questions from one-ten.

How comfortable are you with your own anger?

    1   2   3   4   5   6   7   8   9   10

How comfortable are you with other people's anger?

    1   2   3   4   5   6   7   8   9   10

How much anger do you feel?

    1   2   3   4   5   6   7   8   9   10

How much hurt do you feel?

    1   2   3   4   5   6   7   8   9   10

How flooded with feeling are you?

    1   2   3   4   5   6   7   8   9   10

How angry are you about the fact that you're angry?

    1   2   3   4   5   6   7   8   9   10

How depressed do you feel around your anger?

    1   2   3   4   5   6   7   8   9   10

How overtly aggressive do you become?

    1   2   3   4   5   6   7   8   9   10

How passive aggressive do you become?

    1   2   3   4   5   6   7   8   9   10

How much does your anger affect your intimate relationships?

    1   2   3   4   5   6   7   8   9   10

How much does your anger affect your career?

    1   2   3   4   5   6   7   8   9   10

How good are you at dealing with your anger in healthy ways?

    1   2   3   4   5   6   7   8   9   10

How comfortable are you with the way you deal with your anger?

    1   2   3   4   5   6   7   8   9   10

How much does anger disrupt your life?

    1   2   3   4   5   6   7   8   9   10

Anger Map

Instructions: In the center of the circle, write a word or two describing a current situation or a type of situation that often makes you angry. Next, on the jutting lines write any association you have that comes to mind – that gets triggered by the central circumstance.

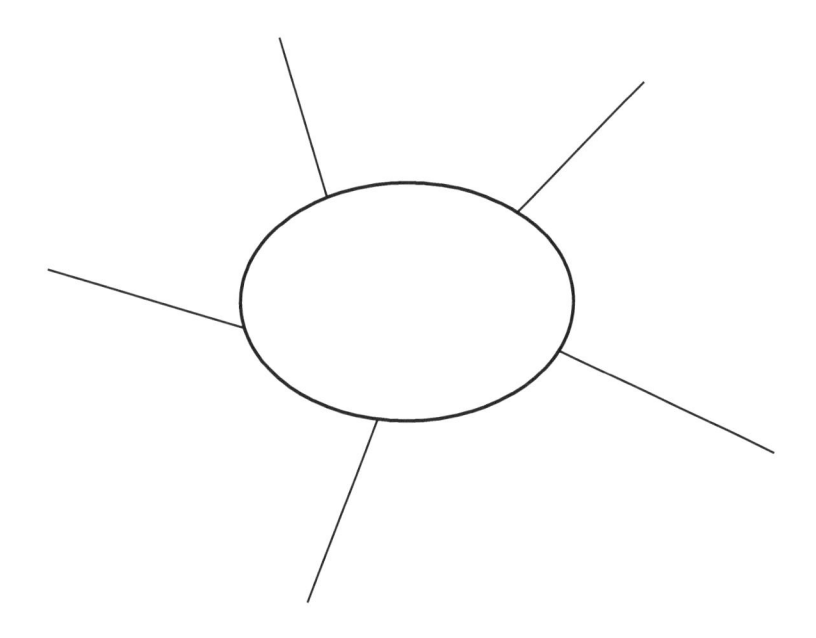

Ask yourself these questions:

What do you notice about your anger that hadn't occurred to you before?

_____
_____
_____

What old anger do you feel might be impacting your life today?

_____
_____
_____

How is anger negatively impacting your life today?

_____
_____
_____

How does your anger express itself? Describe how your form of anger plays out in your life today. (i.e.: Constant criticism, sarcasm, rage, stonewalling, passive aggressive behaviors, controlling, collapsing, whining, acting out behaviors, violence, stonewalling, withdrawal, cut off, coldness manipulation, pushiness, etc.)

_____
_____
_____

What is your anger telling you about areas in which you feel vulnerable or out of control that get easily triggered?

_____
_____
_____

What unresolved pain do you think might be fueling your anger?

_____
_____
_____

What changes in your thinking, feeling life and behavior can you make to bring your anger into better balance?

_____
_____
_____

Exploring Repetitive Patterns

Think of a circumstance in a relationship, either intimate or professional, that tends to repeat itself over and over again in your life and in which you end up feeling hurt or angry.

Notice if there is any pattern to the situation.

_____
_____
_____

Does the pattern repeat itself?

_____
_____
_____

How do you behave?

_____
_____
_____

Do you get angry when you feel hurt?

_____
_____
_____

Do you cry when you get angry?

_____
_____
_____

Do you act as if you are angry at the other person, but secretly feel self-blame and self-doubt?

_____
_____
_____

Journal Entry A:

Write out all the angry feelings that you have felt toward a particular person but never expressed to that person. Example: "I am angry at you because you ...." etc. Give your feelings full vent.

_____
_____
_____
_____
_____
_____

As you read over what you wrote, ask yourself:

Are these unexpressed feelings toward someone from your past being vented onto people in your life today, or possibly onto yourself?

_____
_____
_____

If you are venting them onto yourself, how do you do that?

_____
_____
_____

If you are venting them onto others, is it possible that you are looking for an excuse to let go of built-up tension from unresolved past issues? And if so, what issues?

_____
_____
_____

Journaling Exercises

Exercise: Letting the Child Speak

One journaling exercise that can be useful here is to reverse roles with yourself at any moment in your own childhood where you feel you may have felt disempowered, disconnected, unheard. Journal in the voice of yourself at that time. Journal as the child within you. Talk from that place. Then journal about what fears you may have developed about relationships that you might still be living out today. Use extra paper if necessary.

_____
_____
_____
_____
_____
_____
_____
_____

Exercise: A Moment of Repair

Journal about a time when repair of an angry breech or incident occurred; how you felt afterward within the relationship and what positive lessons you learned about relationship repair from it that you might still be living out today.

_____
_____
_____
_____
_____
_____
_____
_____

Consider ways in which pent-up feelings from the past may be causing you to behave toward others in a way that is not consistent with the real you. Writing in the first person, write a monologue from that part of you that you are trying to hide, the one you don't want anyone to see. Example, "I am Julie and I am small and frightened. Because I'm scared, I act certain ways." When you're finished, read over your monologue. It will help you to understand better how a past painful situation might have made you feel about yourself, because you feared what someone else felt about you.

_____
_____
_____
_____
_____
_____
_____
_____

Chapter 12
Finding Forgiveness

In this chapter you will be exploring the myths surrounding forgiveness, recognizing that forgiveness is a process not an event, identifying where you are in your process and writing letters of forgiveness as a healing journaling exercise.

Myths Surrounding Forgiveness

Which myths do you identify with? Describe why.

If I forgive, my relationship with the person I'm forgiving will definitely improve.

_____
_____
_____

If I forgive, it means I'm condoning the behavior of the person I'm forgiving.

_____
_____
_____

If I forgive, I'll no longer feel angry at the person for what happened.

_____
_____
_____

If I forgive, I forgo my right to hurt feelings.

_____
_____
_____

If I forgive, it means I want to continue to have a relationship with the person I'm forgiving.

_____
_____
_____

If I haven't forgotten, I haven't really forgiven.

_____
_____
_____

I only need to forgive once.

_____
_____
_____

I forgive for the sake of the other person.

_____
_____
_____

Forgiving myself is selfish or wrong.

_____
_____
_____

Stages or Process of Forgiveness

Which stage along the forgiveness process do you feel you are in? Describe.
from *The Magic of Forgiveness*, Tian Dayton

Waking Up: Becoming aware that there is a forgiveness issue to be addressed.

_____
_____
_____

Anger and Resentment: Unresolved anger and resentment that block your ability to forgive.

_____
_____
_____

Sadness and Hurt: Unresolved sadness and hurt that block your ability to forgive.

_____
_____
_____

Integration and Letting Go: Integrating heretofore banished emotions and gaining insight and understanding so that moving on is possible.

_____
_____
_____

Reinvestment: Having worked through emotional pain and anger, you have new energy to invest as you choose.

_____
_____
_____

Letter Writing

Note: These letters are for your eyes only. They are a journaling exercise meant to free you. They are not meant to be sent to anyone. Use extra paper if necessary.

Try writing a letter:

To yourself at some other time in your life, forgiving yourself for something around which you carry pain and shame.

_____
_____
_____
_____
_____
_____
_____
_____

To someone else, forgiving them for hurting you.

_____
_____
_____
_____
_____
_____
_____
_____

Asking for another person's forgiveness.

A letter you wish you had received from someone asking you for your forgiveness.

Chapter 13
Building Resilience

In this chapter you will be identifying the qualities of resilience that you possess, looking back on how you developed resilience throughout your life and exploring ways to build further resilience.

Qualities of Resilience

How many of these qualities of resilience do you feel you possess? Give them a rating from 1-10 as to how much of the quality you feel you possess.

Independence

    1   2   3   4   5   6   7   8   9   10

Creativity

    1   2   3   4   5   6   7   8   9   10

Relationships

    1   2   3   4   5   6   7   8   9   10

Insight

    1   2   3   4   5   6   7   8   9   10

Humor

    1   2   3   4   5   6   7   8   9   10

Morality

    1   2   3   4   5   6   7   8   9   10

Initiative

    1   2   3   4   5   6   7   8   9   10

Describe how your highest and lowest rated qualities affect or play out in your life.

_____
_____
_____

Is there any particular quality that you feel plays an especially important role for you? Explain.

_____
_____
_____

Is there any particular quality that you would like to work to expand in your life? Explain.

_____
_____
_____

What were the resilient attitudes that you recall having as a child?

_____
_____
_____

Did you believe that your life would work out?

_____
_____
_____

Did you believe that you deserved to have a good life?

_____
_____
_____

Who were those special people who helped you to feel good about yourself?

_____
_____

Which of the following characteristics do you identify with and why?

In their research, Wolin and Wolin discovered that resilient children tended to have:

Likable personalities from birth that attracted parents, surrogates and mentors to want to care for them. They were naturally adept recruiters of support and interest from others and drank up attention, care and support from wherever they could get it. Is this you? Describe.

_____
_____
_____

They tended to be of at least average intelligence reading on or above grade level. Is this you? Describe.

_____
_____
_____

Few had another child born within two years of their birth. Is this you? Describe.

_____
_____
_____

Virtually all of the children had at least one person with whom they had developed a strong relationship, often from the extended family or close community member. Did you have this person? If so, who was it and what was your relationship to them like?

_____
_____
_____

Often they report having an inborn feeling that their lives were going to work out. If you identify with this, explain how.

_____
_____
_____

They can identify the illness in their family and are able to find ways to distance themselves from it, they don't let the family dysfunction destroy them. If you identify with this explain how you insulated yourself or distanced yourself from the family illness.

_____
_____
_____

They work through their problems but don't tend to make that a lifestyle. Is this you? Describe.

_____
_____
_____

They take active responsibility for creating their own successful lives. Is this you? Describe.

_____
_____
_____

They tend to have constructive attitudes toward themselves and their lives. If this is you, what are some of those attitudes?

_____
_____
_____

They tend not to fall into self-destructive life styles. Is this you? Describe.

_____
_____
_____

Journaling Exercises

What were your personal strengths that helped you to deal with adversity and how are you using those strengths in your life today?

_____
_____
_____
_____
_____
_____
_____

Write a letter to someone special thanking them for the role they played in your life.

_____
_____
_____
_____
_____
_____
_____

Reverse roles with that person and write a letter from them to you describing what they saw in you.

_____
_____
_____
_____
_____
_____
_____

Chapter 14

Finding Ways to Feel Good Naturally

In this chapter you will be identifying which activities you can engage in that will enhance your recovery and your quality of life.

Which of these natural highs do you have in your life right now?
Place a check in the appropriate box.

- ☐ Exercise/Yoga
- ☐ Breath Awareness
- ☐ Massage
- ☐ Proper Rest and Quiet Time
- ☐ Thinking Positive Thoughts
- ☐ Reading Uplifting Literature
- ☐ Watching Uplifting Films
- ☐ Journaling
- ☐ Creative Visualization
- ☐ Regular Relaxation
- ☐ Meditation
- ☐ Warm Baths
- ☐ Sharing with Others
- ☐ Thirty Minutes of Sunlight Daily
- ☐ Good Nutrition

Which of these natural highs and self-soothers would you like to experience more of?

_____
_____
_____
_____

Where do you feel blocked in enjoying these activities?

_____
_____
_____
_____

What are your favorite self soothers?

_____
_____
_____
_____

How do you generally bring yourself back into balance when you fall out of it?

_____
_____
_____
_____

What changes do you need to make in your life in order to create more emotional sobriety in your life?

_____
_____
_____
_____

Chapter 15
Building My Recovery Network

In this chapter you will be taking active steps to build a recovery network and safety net into your life today.

Following are the building blocks of your recovery network.

- Twelve-Step Recovery
- Good Nutrition
- Healthy Exercise
- Body Work
- One-to-One Therapy
- Group Therapy
- Hobbies
- Sprituality/Community

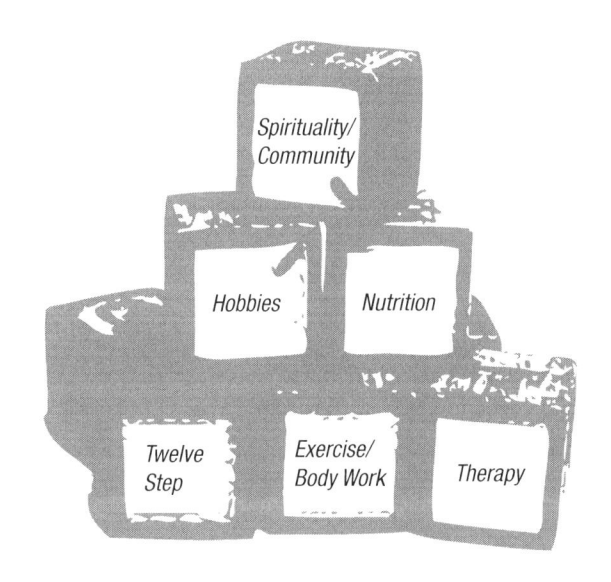

Which of these building blocks do you have in place?
_____
_____
_____

Which of these building blocks do you need to put into place?
_____
_____
_____

Which of these areas are you feeling blocked in?

_____
_____
_____

Why do you imagine you are blocked?

_____
_____
_____

Which areas are moving along nicely?

_____
_____
_____

How would you like your recovery network to look?

_____
_____
_____

What feelings does it bring up in you to have your network where you'd like it to be?

_____
_____
_____
_____
_____
_____

Chapter 16

Making Changes
Exploring a Specific Life Role

In this chapter you will be looking at the roles in your life, exploring your level of satisfaction or dissatisfaction in them and figuring out which roles you want to change, play more of or play less of in order to achieve emotional sobriety and balance.

Life Roles

Thinking, Feeling and Behavior are role-specific. We think, feel and behave according to and shaped by a role we're playing. When we examine the role we can explore its interior thoughts, feelings and behaviors. Healthy people have a balance of roles in life that they move in and out of. When we move through life changes, we may add new roles and let go of or allow some to be dormant.

Explore and answer these questions.

Are the roles in your life balanced?

_____
_____
_____

Which roles dominate? Which roles are overplayed in your life? (i.e.: mother, father, worker, addict, exerciser, parent and so on)

_____
_____
_____

Which roles are too small or underplayed in your life?

_____
_____
_____

Which roles do you feel most alive in?

_____
_____
_____

Which roles do you feel most shut down in?

_____
_____
_____

If you could magically add a role to your life, what role would you add?

_____
_____
_____

If you could magically shrink a role, which one would it be?

_____
_____
_____

Now choose a role that you would either like to increase or decrease in your life and answer the following questions "as" that role. (i.e.: I would like to add the role of "playful person" or "successful worker"; I would like to lessen the role of "angry person" or overeater" and so on)

How much time do you spend in this role? (i.e.: I spend two thirds of my life in "overeater" – some of it actually eating and the rest obsessing about food)

_____
_____
_____

How much satisfaction do you experience?

_____
_____
_____

How much fatigue or burnout?

_____
_____
_____

How much success?

_____
_____
_____

How much failure?

_____
_____
_____

What would the role like to say to you? (i.e.: as overeater, I would like to tell you that I am controlling a lot of your life, I am in the driver's seat)

_____
_____
_____

What would you like to say back to the role?

_____
_____
_____

How might you adjust or change the role to better suit you?

_____
_____

Undeveloped Roles

Name a role that you would like to develop further:

What is the role?

_____
_____
_____

What draws you to this role?

_____
_____
_____

What parts of yourself do you feel would be actualized by playing this role?

_____
_____
_____

What strengths do you bring to this role?

_____
_____
_____

What are your weaknesses in this role?

_____
_____
_____

What might you have to give up to play this role?

_____
_____
_____

What might you gain in playing this role?

_____
_____
_____

> **Write a mission statement of about ten lines for your life.**
> (i.e.: I am Manny and these are my values and goals for my life now and in the future.)
>
> _____
> _____
> _____
> _____
> _____
> _____
> _____
> _____
> _____
> _____
> _____
> _____

Made in the USA
Middletown, DE
06 December 2014